the Stick & the Stone

By Joel Pankow & Jonathan Mayer

Illustrated by Jonathan Mayer

A very long time ago, near the Desert of Sinai, many thousands of people were walking slowly across the dry, rocky ground. The robes that they wore were old and dirty. Their skin was brown, and all the men had dark beards. They had with them carts and wagons, herds of animals, and everything they owned. They were the nation of Israel, God's chosen people. It was getting late in the day, and all the people looked tired and hungry.

A tall, white cloud moved ahead of the Israelites. Just before sunset, the cloud stopped moving, and it set its tail on the ground. Then a horn sounded. The Israelites stopped walking and set up their tents for the night. Soon the cloud would turn to fire to give them light during the night.

Levi was glad they had stopped. He wasn't as tired as his parents and four older brothers, because he was allowed to ride on the cart for most of the day. While his father and brothers began to build a fire, Levi took the long stick he had found that day and skipped off to find his cousins. Maybe they would want to play swords with him.

Just then, he heard his mother call, "Levi!"

Levi stopped and turned to face his mother. "Yes, mother?"

"Don't wander too far. Be back at the tent by supper time."

Levi nodded. "Yes, mother." Then he darted off between tents to find his cousins.

Levi's cousins were usually ahead of his family, so he ran a little ways toward the front of the camp. After looking for some time, he didn't find his cousins' tent. He got closer to the front of the camp, until finally he reached the very edge of it. His relatives were nowhere to be seen. He must have passed right by them.

Just as Levi was turning to go back, he saw a man walking alone away from the camp. He was going toward the pillar of cloud. It was beginning to get dark, and Levi knew he should be back at his family's tent soon. He wanted to see what this strange man was up to, though. He decided to follow him from a distance.

Levi quietly got a little closer. He saw that the man was very big, older than his father, with a tall staff that was bent at the top. He had a large beard and shaggy, dark hair. The man suddenly stopped, turned, and looked right at Levi from beneath his bushy eyebrows. Just then, the pillar of cloud began to glow like a hot furnace. Levi ran for his life!

The young boy was out of breath when he got back to his family's tent.

"You're just in time for supper," his mother said. "What are you so excited about?"

"I saw an old man!" Levi said, puffing for breath. "He was huge, with a big beard and a tall staff. And he looked right at me!"

Levi's father handed him a cake of manna that had been baked by the fire. "Sit down and eat your supper. You must have met Moses."

Levi's eyes got even wider. "That was Moses? The one who led us out of Egypt?"

"It must be him," said Levi's older brother, Caleb. "I've never seen anyone as old as Moses look so big and strong."

"And the staff you saw?" said Levi's mother. "That must have been the same staff that parted the Red Sea."

Levi was speechless. He was glad that Moses hadn't caught him. He might have been turned into a goat! He nibbled at his manna until it was gone, then he went into the tent. He rolled out his blankets next to his brothers and tried to go to sleep.

The next morning, Levi helped his family gather manna from the ground. They took enough to last them only one day. After eating some for breakfast, they packed up their tent and got ready to leave again.

Today, Levi didn't want to ride in the cart. He wanted to get a better look at Moses. When the cloud lifted its tail and started moving again, Levi ran on ahead of his family. He brought his trusty stick along for protection. For hours, he slowly worked his way up to the front of the crowd. Finally, Levi saw him.

He was almost as big as Levi remembered, and walking a short way out in front of everyone else. Levi tried to stay hidden among the people and animals near the front while he watched Moses. Sometimes Moses would look back over his shoulder, and Levi would hop behind a wagon cart so that he wouldn't be seen.

But this time, when Levi looked around the cart, he didn't see Moses out in front anymore.

Suddenly, a deep voice came from behind him. "Boy, come walk with me."

Levi jumped. When he turned around, it was Moses behind him!

"Come along now," said Moses with a gentle smile. "I won't hurt you. But if you keep standing there, you'll be flattened."

Moses went on ahead of the crowd again, and Levi timidly caught up to him.

"What's your name, son?" Moses asked.

"Levi," he replied with a small voice.

"Well, Levi, is there something that you want to ask me?"

Levi swallowed as he looked up at the big man. "Are you really the one who led us out of Egypt?"

Moses shook his head. "No, I'm not."

Levi looked confused. "But aren't you Moses?"

"Yes," Moses said. "But I didn't lead us out of Egypt." He pointed up ahead of them to the cloud. "God led us out."

"Oh," said Levi, peering up at the cloud. He had never been this close to it before, and somehow it seemed scarier knowing that the Lord was inside of it. He suddenly noticed Moses' staff again, and then brightened. "Then is this the staff that parted the Red Sea?"

Again, Moses shook his head. "Oh, I'm afraid the staff didn't have anything to do with that."

"Why not?" asked the boy.

"Because it's only a stick, just like the one you have," said Moses with a smile.

Levi looked at his little stick, then back at the big staff. "But mine's not magic," he said.

"Neither is this one," replied Moses. "But the Lord is very powerful, and he worked the miracles through this staff."

"You mean, like the plagues in Egypt?" Levi asked.

"Yes, and many other miracles," said Moses.

"When God first sent me to the Pharaoh, he gave me a sign so that they would believe that God really sent me. He told me to throw this staff down on the ground. When I did, the staff became a big snake."

Levi quickly stepped away from Moses. "If you drop your staff, does it still turn into a snake?"

"No," replied Moses. "It only happened when God said it would happen. See?" Moses threw the staff onto the ground in front of them. Nothing happened.

Levi ran ahead to pick it up. He looked closely at the staff. It was well worn, with many dents and scratches in it. "But why would God want to do miracles with this old piece of wood?"

Moses just smiled as he took the staff again. "That's a good question, but only God knows the answer." He nodded his head toward the crowd following behind him. "Why would the Lord want us to be his chosen people?"

Levi thought the answer was simple. "Because we're special," he said proudly.

Moses shook his head with a sad look in his eyes. "No, I'm afraid we're all very sinful. On our own, we are only selfish and unkind. If we are special, it is only because God chose to love us."

The boy looked down at the ground as he thought about it. He knew it was true. He could remember dozens of times when he had disobeyed his parents, lied, or was cruel to his brothers. Why would God want him to be his child? "I guess you're right," said Levi quietly.

Moses could sense Levi's guilt. He bent down and picked him up in his big, strong arms, and smiled. "Even though we can't follow God's will perfectly, he forgives us. Day after day he continues to call us his own children. He loves us so much that he promised to pay the price for our sins."

Levi didn't know exactly what that meant, but he was comforted that the Lord had forgiven him. He looked up at the tall cloud in front of them just as it settled down to stop for the day. It didn't seem quite so scary, anymore. And neither did Moses, he decided.

The ram's horn sounded to signal the crowd to stop moving and make camp. "I guess that means I should find my family," said Levi.

Moses set him down on the ground and smiled. "That sounds like a good idea."

Levi smiled back at him, then trotted off into the crowd. He was eager to tell his family about his talk with Moses.

He was still looking for his tribe's banner when a group of angry men started walking towards him. Levi ducked under a wagon until they passed. He heard them grumbling about Moses, so he decided to follow them.

They marched straight to the front of the camp where Moses was making his tent. Levi noticed that some of the men had stones in their hands. "Why are we making camp again where there is no water for us to drink?" they shouted at Moses. "At least in Egypt we had plenty of water. Do you want us and our children to die of thirst?"

Levi realized that he was very thirsty, too. He hadn't had any water since they left camp this morning, and it was only a little. Moses looked like he didn't know what to say. But then he turned away and said, "The Lord will provide." The men shook their fists at him and left, angrier than when they had come.

The boy watched from behind a tent post. Moses went out away from the camp a little ways and knelt down in the dust. He put his head down on the ground and prayed to God, but Levi couldn't hear what he was saying.

After a short while, Moses got up and came back to the camp. He spoke to some men nearby, and one of them blew loudly on a horn three times. The elders of the tribes came to Moses. One of them was Levi's father. Levi jumped out of his hiding place and ran to his father.

"Father!" he shouted.

"Levi, what are you doing here?" his father asked.

"I was talking with Moses, and then some angry men came asking for water," he said. "Then Moses went out to pray, and I think he's going to do something now. May I go with you?"

His father shook his head. "No, Levi. You stay behind." Levi was sad at this news. His father added, "But if you climb up on that rock, you might be able to watch." He smiled, patted his son on the head, and then followed Moses and the other elders out into the desert.

Levi went to the rock his father had pointed to. It was only a stone's throw from the camp, and as tall as two men. He climbed up to the top and sat down to watch.

Moses led the elders out to the middle of the valley, where there was a very large stone sticking up out of the ground. The elders gathered around the stone, and Moses raised his staff into the air. Levi's eyes widened with excitement. He knew God was about to do a miracle with the staff.

Moses hit the stone hard with his staff, and a fountain of water gushed out of it. The water came out so fast that Moses and the

elders had to back away from the rock as the valley began to fill with water. The elders ran back towards the camp with their robes soaking wet. They were shouting to their tribes that the Lord had provided water for them.

Levi quickly climbed down from the rock. He was thirsty, but the very first thing he wanted to do was to run back to his family. He had to tell them how God had saved Israel with a stick and a stone!

Thousands of years after Moses, the Lord has done many miracles through ordinary things. The greatest miracle of all took place in the body of a man hanging on a simple wooden cross. But that ordinary-looking man was also true God—Jesus, our Savior. He was the sacrifice God provided for our sins. Because of Jesus, all of our sin has been taken away.

Even today, God still works miracles through ordinary things. In baptism, the Holy Spirit entered your heart through ordinary water and a few spoken words. Even though there was nothing special about us, God chose to love us and to make us his children. Now we are special because he chose us.

In the Lord's Supper, God forgives our sins because of Jesus' death on the cross. When we eat the bread and drink the wine, Jesus promised that we are also really taking his body and blood.

How wise and wonderful our God is! He works the miracles of faith and forgiveness in the hearts of ordinary people, with such ordinary things. And just like God did many great miracles through a wooden stick, we can be sure that God can do wonderful things for us through his Word and sacraments!

Made in the USA
Monee, IL
02 March 2025

13252108R00019